My World of Science

NATU
MAN

Angela Royston

Heinemann
LIBRARY

www.heinemann.co.uk/library
Visit our website to find out more information about **Heinemann Library** books.

To order:
☎ Phone 44 (0) 1865 888066
▤ Send a fax to 44 (0) 1865 314091
▢ Visit the Heinemann Bookshop at www.heinemann.co.uk/library to browse our catalogue and order online.

First published in Great Britain by Heinemann Library, Halley Court, Jordan Hill, Oxford OX2 8EJ, part of Harcourt Education.

Heinemann is a registered trademark of Harcourt Education Ltd.

© Harcourt Education Ltd 2003
First published in paperback in 2004
The moral right of the proprietor has been asserted.

Editorial: Andrew Farrow and Dan Nunn
Design: Jo Hinton-Malivoire and
    Tinstar Design Limited (www.tinstar.co.uk)
Picture Research: Maria Joannou and Sally Smith
Production: Viv Hichens

Originated by Blenheim Colour Ltd
Printed and bound in China by
    South China Printing Company

ISBN 0 431 13725 0 (hardback)
07 06 05 04 03
10 9 8 7 6 5 4 3 2 1

ISBN 0 431 13731 5 (paperback)
08 07 06 05 04
10 9 8 7 6 5 4 3 2 1

British Library Cataloguing in Publication Data
Royston, Angela
Natural and man-made. – (My world of science)
1. Synthetic products – Juvenile literature
2. Natural products – Juvenile literature
I. Title
620.1'1

A full catalogue record for this book is available from the British Library.

Acknowledgements
The publishers would like to thank the following for permission to reproduce photographs:
Corbis p. **10**; Eye Ubiquitous/Julia Bayne p. **4**; Getty Images p. **25**; Peter Gould p. **8** inset; Photodisc pp. **16**, **20**, **29**; Rupert Horrox pp. **9**, **14**; Still Pictures p. **8**; Trevor Clifford pp. **5**, **6**, **7**, **11**, **12**, **13**, **15**, **17**, **18**, **19**, **21**, **22**, **23**, **24**, **26**, **28**; Trip/D. Rayers p. **27**.

Cover photograph reproduced with permission of Trevor Clifford.

Every effort has been made to contact copyright holders of any material reproduced in this book. Any omissions will be rectified in subsequent printings if notice is given to the publishers.

Contents

Any words appearing in the text in bold, **like this**,
are explained in the Glossary.

What is a natural material?

Natural **materials** come from plants or animals or from the ground. Wood is one kind of natural material. This bench is made out of wood.

These things are made of materials that come from the ground. Metals are found in some rocks. Glass is made from grains of sand.

Some natural materials

Some natural **materials** come from plants. Paper comes from **mashed-up** wood. Cotton comes from fluffy cotton seeds. Which thing is made of rope? (Answer on page 31.)

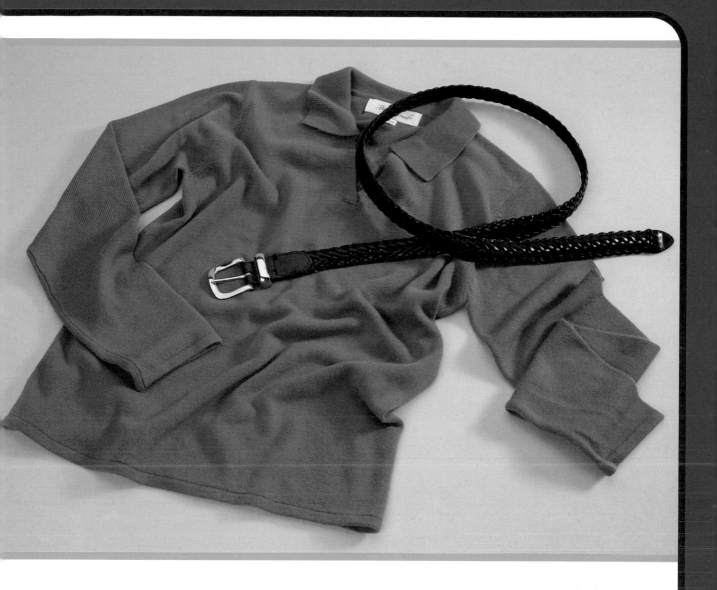

This jersey has been knitted from wool.
Wool comes from the soft **fleece** of
sheep. The belt is made of **leather**.
Leather is made from animal skin.

What is a man-made material?

Man-made **materials** are made from **oil**. Most oil lies deep beneath the ground. **Engineers** drill a deep hole to reach the black, runny oil.

Oil is made into many kinds of
man-made materials. Most of them
do not look like oil in any way!
Plastic is one material made from oil.

Plastic

Plastic can be made into many different shapes. This factory uses **moulds** to make plastic boots. Hot, liquid plastic is poured into each mould. It quickly cools to form the shape of a boot.

Some plastic is very strong. These safety goggles are made of a plastic that is stronger than glass. Plastic can also be very soft, like this doll.

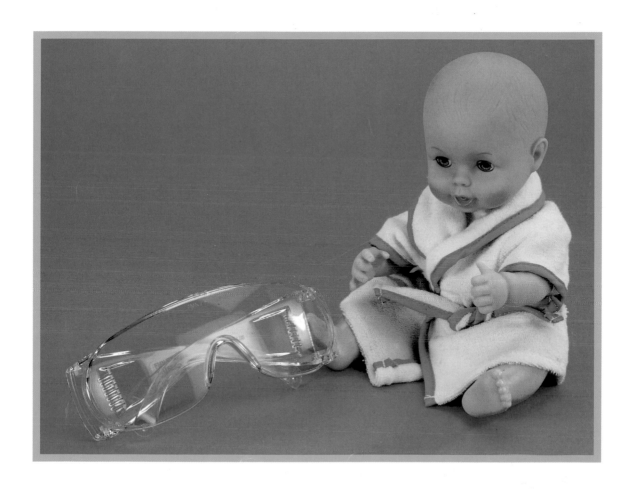

Some man-made materials

These things are all made of plastic.
Some plastic things are hard and
some are bendy. Which of these
things protects your eyes from the
Sun? (Answer on page 31.)

Plastic can be made to look like a natural **material**. These things are made of plastic, but the plastic looks like **leather**. Leather feels softer than plastic.

Glass or plastic?

These bottles are made of glass. Glass is a natural **material** that is quite heavy. But glass cracks and breaks easily.

This bottle and **tumbler** both look like glass but they are made of plastic. Plastic is cheaper than glass. Plastic does not break so easily when it is dropped.

China or plastic?

These plates and cups are made of china. China is a natural **material**. It is a kind of **clay**, which comes from the ground. China breaks easily.

These plates, mugs and flowerpots are made of plastic. Plastic is lighter and cheaper than china. It does not break easily. But it does not feel like china.

Wood, stone or plastic?

The animals have been carved from wood. The statue of the people is made of **marble**. Plastic can be made to look like these natural **materials**.

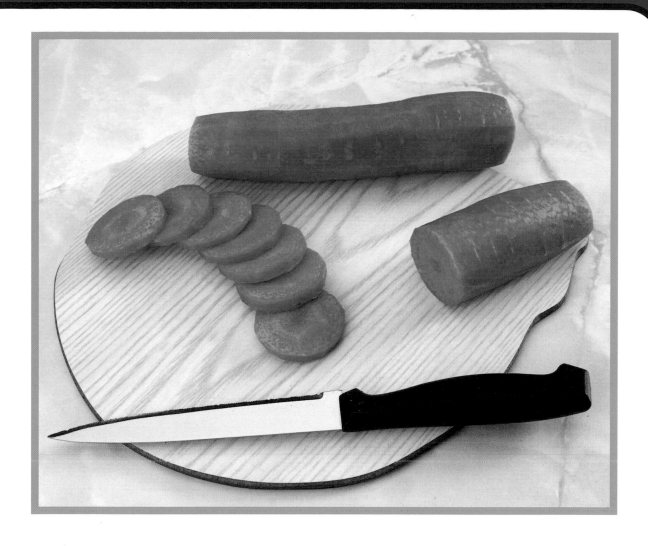

The top of this work surface and the top of this chopping board are both covered with sheets of plastic. Which sheet looks like wood? Which one looks like marble? (Answers on page 31.)

Wax or plastic?

Candles are made of **wax**. The wax is a man-made **material**. When the candle is lit, the wax melts and soaks into the wick. Plastic cannot do this.

The girl is drawing with coloured crayons made of wax. The boy's crayons are made of plastic. The plastic crayons give brighter colours than the wax crayons.

A mixture of materials

Many things contain natural and man-made **materials**. The top parts of these trainers are made of **leather**. The **soles** are made of man-made material.

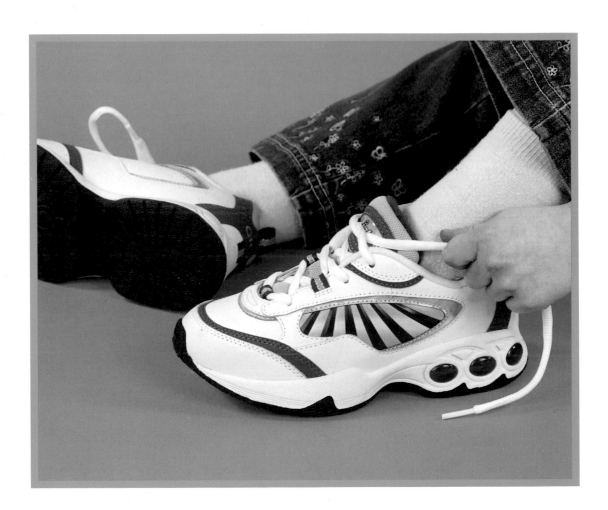

The frame of this bicycle is made of metal. So are the spokes of the wheels. The saddle and the pedals are made of man-made materials.

Clothes

This jumper is made of a mixture of natural and man-made **materials**. The materials are mixed together so well that you cannot tell them apart. Many clothes are like this.

Shirts that contain man-made materials do not crease as much as cotton shirts. This means that they are easier to **iron** smooth.

Warm and windproof

This girl is wearing a warm **fleecy** coat. It is made of man-made **materials**. It keeps her warm but feels light to wear.

Skiers need to wear clothes that keep out the snow and the wind. This girl's special ski trousers, coat and gloves are all made of man-made materials.

Will it rot?

This wooden chair is old and has started to **rot**. The plastic chair will not rot like the wooden chair. This is useful until you want to throw it away!

Natural **materials** slowly rot and become part of the soil. But rubbish tips are filled with things made of plastic that will never rot away.

Glossary

clay a kind of heavy soil

engineer someone who builds things like engines, machines, roads and buildings

fleece the fluffy, woolly hair that covers a sheep

fleecy warm, light and fluffy

iron to use a hot machine to smooth out the crinkles in cloth

leather natural material made from the skin of a cow or other animal

marble a smooth, hard stone

mashed-up squashed and mixed with liquid

material the stuff that something is made of

mould a hollow shape that is filled with liquid. When the liquid cools it becomes a solid with the same shape as the mould.

oil a liquid found in the ground. It is used to make petrol, plastic and other things.

rot slowly break into small pieces

sole the part of the shoe that touches the ground

tumblers tall glasses that are used for drinking water and other liquids

wax a material that is soft when heated. Most wax is made from oil, but some wax is made by bees.

Answers

page 6

The sandals are made of rope.

page 12

The sunglasses protect your eyes
from the Sun.

page 19

The sheet covering the chopping board
looks like wood. The sheet covering the
work surface looks like marble.

Index